An Entrepreneur's Impact

A Memoir of Success

From the Professor Lecture Series

Written by: By: David K. Ewen, M.Ed.

Published by: Ewen Prime Company

Audiobook Narration by: David K. Ewen, M.Ed.

Educational services by Forest Academy

Broadcast services by Your World Discovered

Copyright Notice

An Entrepreneur's Impact

A Memoir of Success

By: David K. Ewen, M.Ed.

ISBN-13: 978-1535111423
ISBN-10: 1535111429

An Entrepreneur's Impact
A Memoir of Success

By:

David K. Ewen, M.Ed.

Ewen Prime Company

Forest Academy

Your World Discovered

Kelvin Projects

EPN & EPN News

"For I know the plans I have for you," declares the Lord, "plans to prosper you and not to harm you, plans to give you hope and a future."

- Jeremiah 29:11 (NIV)

"I ask God to lead me toward the lasting legacy that He wants me to leave behind on this world we call Earth."

- David K., Ewen, M.Ed. (July 2016)

The Cover of Memoir

A memoir documents the legacy that is intended to be left behind. The logo of Forest Academy, one moniker of my entrepreneurial experiences, is that of the world being seen in space. This also is the cover of this memoir. My goal is to have a positively resulting impact on the world that we live in. This is what I want to leave behind. I ask God to lead me toward the lasting legacy that He wants me to leave behind on this world we call Earth.

We all have a contribution to give. This memoir avoids prideful boastful language and puts greater attention on a revelation of what years of work accomplishes. After decades of contribution, it can reach international levels. This is a global contribution that is worth leaving behind.

Contents

- Memoir
- Intended Legacy
- Who is David Ewen
- Story of Paper Books
- Ewen Prime Company
- Other Businesses
- Broadcasting Ventures
- The Early Years
- Forest Academy
- Professor Lecture Series
- Knowing My Audience
- My Staff
- Honored to Meet People
- Describing My Contribution
- Over the Years
- Making an Impact
- Other Media Outlets

- The First Tour
- Being On the Map
- Christian Influence
- Relevant Scriptures
- The Future
- Conclusion

<u>Dedication</u>

I dedicate this memoir to everyone who has come aboard Ewen Prime Company in one fashion or another and has taken part in the voyage of exploration of entrepreneurial studies and digital multimedia technology. Those people include the authors editors and illustrators who were part of the first set of public works in the mid-1990s. It also includes the Independent Publishers of New England, currently in operation, which was originally founded with the seeds planted by the New England Publishers Association launched in May of 1998 at the offices of Ewen Prime Company in Natick Massachusetts. I also give dedication to the audience of my lectures at the universities, colleges and educational institutions in the seven states of New York and New England. Finally, I give thanks to my listeners of my radio broadcasts and viewers of my television shows. The countless number of people that have been part of my entrepreneurial voyage have supported my passion that allows me to share my story.

By the time I met my wife in 2002, I had already been in business for eight years. She has been the strongest support that I have had from that time forward. You may have heard the expression that behind every successful man is a strong supportive woman. That is who my wife is to me. She has been with me at radio stations, lecture halls, and festival events as part of her voyage with me every step of the way.

I have a strong belief that my family that I grew up in played a strong part in my development growing up. There were a lot of people involved as I was one of eight family siblings and two loving parents. Of course there was the dog that was fun too.

I believe that everyone that I interfaced with at home, school, social life, and in my professional career had an influence on me. As the expression goes, I am a sum of all of my experiences. This is something I truly believe in. It is impossible to give dedication to every person who I came across. most assuredly they all had a positive impact in my life even at times where it may have felt as a negative impact. Every negative impact makes us stronger for a future positive impact. Granted it may be painful, but they are all beneficial in the long term. If you lived experiences with learning through growth, then the success that comes out of these experiences can be realized and recognized.

"For I know the plans I have for you," declares the Lord, "plans to prosper you and not to harm you, plans to give you hope and a future."

- Jeremiah 29:11 (NIV)

For the Record

This memoir is a matter of record and a testimony showing that hard work and perseverance driven by passion results in good things. It also includes an understanding that a faith in our God and His will is incorporated into successful elements of people's lives. I did not know this in my early stages of my entrepreneurial career, but after nearly a quarter of a century of experience, this has been proven to be evident.

This memoir is not intended to be boastful or evoke a sense of pride. It is a story of truth of revelations learned over time.

Ewen Prime Company launched in July of 1994 and this memoir is the story that talks about the journey over a 22-year period of entrepreneurship and business adventurism. The business has been a vehicle of exploration of human entrepreneurial spirit and an adventure involving contacts along the way.

Goal of Memoir

The goal of this memoir is to show an entrepreneur's impact showing a legacy of success that comes from persevering and not giving up.   Starting a business is not easy and only the financially successful ones are what most people know about.   Every entrepreneur has dreams of growth and financial success that comes from thinking big.   This visible manifestation of business ownership is what every entrepreneur dreams of.

What people do not see is the sweat and hard work that is driven by persevering passion that most people do not understand.   This concept is often lost in telling the story of launching a business.   This leads others to think if they have a good idea for a business, then amazing flourishing businesses will come about.   Unfortunately, this isn't true. Many businesses go through a phase of trial in which they will either succeed or fail. This is story of a success shown by the connections to many people along the way.

This is not a boastful or prideful story. It is by no means intended to boost up pride or tell stories to be boastful about. This should not be perceived in that way.

As we grow older, we become wiser in a way that take complicated ideas and put them into perspective so that they become simple. An example is to look for solutions to problems rather than implement solutions to problems that don't exist. Many novice-entrepreneurs do not take problems and work out a solution. Before getting to that point, they miss what the problem is. Instead, they come up with solutions that are looking for problems. When this is done complexities take place.   These kinds of people focus on finding creative solutions when they are not needed.   A wise person can first discern what a true problem is and then applying a solution to that identified problem.   This sound simple, but novice-entrepreneurs sometimes struggle to understand this. I know because I was a novice-entrepreneur who thought I had all the answers.   What I didn't realize at the time was that some of those answers weren't needed as they did not apply to a real problem.   It took evolution of thought that helped me to recognize a problem and what should be done about it. In some cases, doing nothing is the right choice. It is hard for a novice-entrepreneur to accept not doing anything as a right answer.

Another goal of this memoir is to teach how to communicate.   The Bible tells us to be quick to listen and slow to speak (James 1:19). This means we should seek first to understand and then to be understood as author Stephen R. Covey says in his book "Seven Habits of Highly Effective People". The actual quote from his book reads: "Seek first to understand, then to be understood".

<u>Point in Time</u>

The point in time that this memoir is released is Sunday, July 24, 2016. My journey as an entrepreneur began on Wednesday, July 24, 1994 at 11:30 am. On the release of this memoir on July 24, 2016, I commemorate 22 years in business as an entrepreneur, publisher, broadcaster, talk show host, filmmaker, lecturer, author, speaker, and publicist.

This career memoir marks a specific time period in my life where I worked as an entrepreneur during the years of 1994, from when I first launched my business, to 22 years later on the anniversary of the business on July 24th 2016. This Memoir is being released on July 24th 2016 to recognize 22 years of a passion of entrepreneurial spirit with a vision and mission in mind that has remained the same.

Although I have worked for other businesses as an employee along the years, this memoir specifically makes note of my personal entrepreneurial experiences as a business owner and contributor to my community and the world I live in.

The most important legacy a person has is what they leave behind and for me it is my contribution produced through my entrepreneurial ventures as a business owner. It is the trail of success stories and testimonies that I will leave behind.

This memoir of entrepreneurial experiences formerly documents 22 years in the form of a montage of memories that's spread across various industries with skills and abilities developed over time. I do expect that this same style of evolution to continue for the next 22 years.

I thought it timely to mark the midway point with memories that expanded across the equivalent of the time if one generation.   So much happens in one generation and I thought it best to report on this specific duration of a generation time period.

I was 30 years old when I started developing the business plan for my business and entrepreneurial venture. At 31, I finally launched Ewen Prime Company on July 24, 1994. this Memoir is being written when I am 53 years old. You can imagine the difference between a 31-year-old and the experiential knowledge above 53-year-old. This memoir document that evolution of accomplishment driven by passion.   The year this memoir was written is

2016. A lot has happened since 1994. A lot can happen in a generation. This isn't the end. The journey is planned to continue for another generation. So much will happen in the future 22 years that it is best to clearly document and recognize the appreciation of the previous 22 years.

The point in time of this memoir is July 24, 2016 after 22 years in business. The next 22 years will do more with entrepreneurial studies, business adventurism, digital multimedia technologies, and education. All of that can certainly evolve in 22 years as has already been shown in the last 22 years. I'm excited to see what the future will bring. The excitement comes from a tsunami of opportunity that has flowed my way over the past 22 years. I anticipate much greater things to come.

Where I Am From

I was born in Boston with my twin sister and grew up in the town of Weston, Massachusetts with a total of 7 siblings. I graduated from Weston High School before moving on to college at the University of Massachusetts in Amherst Massachusetts. I received my master's degree in education in 1988 at Cambridge College in Cambridge, Massachusetts. I launched my business in July of 1994 in Natick, Massachusetts.

The expansion of my business from Natick, Massachusetts moved to Westborough, Massachusetts after having reached coverage in the New England states following the launch of the New England Publishers Association.

The business expanded from book publishing to other digital multimedia and educational products and services. The geographic area that I cover now includes Japan, China, the Middle East and the United States. Today my entrepreneurial experience is international. Nearly a quarter-century ago it was intended to only be local to Natick, Massachusetts. A lot has happened in nearly a quarter of a century.

My physical presence has been primarily Massachusetts with original representation within the New England States. Today, the representation has reached around the word in the form of an educational ambassadorship that shares culture.

<u>Being Successful</u>

Being successful does not necessarily mean financial success. I wouldn't much rather be at peace when I go home with a loving wife then to be alone and wealthy. My discussion in "An Entrepreneur's Impact" is related to my entrepreneurial experience as a business person who worked with many wonderful people and that profitability was in the positive area.

When I talk about profitability, I am not talking about making huge sums of money. My definition of profitability is making correct business decisions that steer away from the death of a business and that there is some level of profitability. That is success. It is a reality. I have been fortunate to discover ways to have a return on investment on decisions. There were good choices that avoided bad consequences. Many of those investment choices were a zero-dollar amount small return. What is important is that the return on investment is positive and not negative. That is the result of effective decision-making practices that shows business-safety, economic conservativeness, and forethought.

When I talk about being successful and having a positive return on investment, that doesn't mean I was always successful and always had a positive return on investment. In more than two decades, I have made all the mistakes possible however recovered from them and learned how to make good business decisions for the future. A very well-known minister by the name of Bishop T.D. Jakes explains that the journey is more important than the destination. The destination is the result of having a good journey and that in turn determines success. If the journey is the result of poor practices and poor methodologies, then the destination will result and a terrible end point. It is important to learn from mistakes and receive necessary guidance to head towards the direction of success.

Passion

The work that I have done as an entrepreneur and business person is the result of the passion I have for the work that I do in the world around me and around others. That passion is what drove me to not give up during the most difficult times in my earlier business career as I was learning. Not many people know my early years in business and how I behaved with the lack of experience as an entrepreneur. It makes sense. They didn't walk with me during my early business career. Today, people see me make decisions and give advice based on more than two decades' experience and revelation overtime. This is what people see and recognize today. They have the perception that I always had the right answers to all entrepreneurial challenges in business. They see me as I am today and not what I evolved from in the past. I fully understand that as I have lectured on multiple business topics at universities and colleges and published many books on the topic. However, that is not what the beginning looked like so many years ago.

A pastor friend of mine, Jose Martinez, (my spiritual father) has used the expression to describe historical growth by saying that there is a story to the glory. Behind every glory there is a story that involves hard work and determination. That hard work and determination is what defines the result of passion. With passion the only result is determination and hard work which leads to a positive outcome.

When I started in business in 1994 and struggled for the first five to ten years, I had several opportunities to give up and leave the industry. I did not. I kept going. I kept working on finding new ways to do things. My effort was toward researching in discovering improvements in the ways I was doing things. As I would reach a new level, I would continue to research to get to the next level after that. After nearly a quarter of a century, people have seen the result of that effort, however do not know what that effort involved.

Lecture Introduction

During my public speaking lectures, I tend to spend a few minutes introducing my background so that my audience understands why I say certain things and instruct people to do certain things. This content is an opportunity to share a more detailed understanding of the experience acquired over more than two decades. It is a collage of memoir related events that help depict what is inside my head to provide understanding of how I developed as an entrepreneur over many years.

A person can give another person advice but it may not be accepted if it's not understood the foundation of where that advice is coming from. Accepting advice, without knowing that it comes from experience and fact, is harder to accept.

For whatever reasons, successful business people choose to make decisions based on a gut feeling that is related to desires and not the strong order of experience and facts. When the judgment is found to be incorrect, the only good that comes out of it is that a learning opportunity is received. If it is not received, then continual mistakes will be made. Fortunately, I learned very early on in my entrepreneurial career to learn from my mistakes. The biggest mistake was to follow gut instinct that was based on assumptions, false opinions, and feelings. In the beginning, it was not based on structured logic and experience. Fortunately, years have passed that has developed experience now incorporated in my decision making process. The expression that older is wiser is true. I don't see any exception. Experience does develop wisdom. There are many ways to succeed in life. Of course a formal education is important. Another door way is using experience in a positive way that retains the recognition of good and bad choices.

My Story

For about the first 15 years of my working career, I worked in information technology in large data processing environments for financial institutions. I loved it. But this is not where my story begins. My story begins when I became an entrepreneur to provide a contribution in the world that I live in. That contribution has to do with media content delivery to the general public. When I began in book publishing, it was believed that only large publishing houses could be successful. My earlier efforts in business proved that to be wrong. This was due to a lack of experience. It was hard for many people to take me seriously as a business-person because I did not display the fruits of experience. That experience is developed over time and did not exist during my early years in business.

I didn't want to make mistakes, but I did. I didn't want to spend money on the wrong investments, but I did. I didn't want to make the wrong choices, but I did. Over time, I created a mental library of mistakes and used them to steer me toward the right choices. For me, it was the best way to learn. Yes, it was a cost, but it worked. For others, I find this to be true. My advice is not always taken, because the right choice doesn't always sound like the right choice.

It is funny how the right choice, as logical it may be, does not seem like the right choice to a novice-entrepreneur. Even with testimonies of success and experience, a novice-entrepreneur feels they have the better knowledge. I recognized that and respect that. I too made that same mistake. I suppose, many entrepreneurs need to evolve through mistakes and miss-steps. It worked for me, so it may work for others. Fortunately, in my case, I was not discouraged and I persevered to move forward to reach accomplishment.

Now with experience of nearly a quarter of a century, I see new business owners and entrepreneurs ignore my advice and spend hundreds and thousands of dollars related to poor decisions. It seems, many novice-entrepreneurs have the belief that investing money brings in money. That does not always hold true, especially if the choice of investment is simply wrong.

The wrong investment is a trial-by-error approach almost like gambling and novice-entrepreneurs forget that "the house always wins".   I was one of those people in my early years in business.   As an experienced seasoned professional businessman, I now look back with regret in one way and satisfaction in another way.   My satisfaction comes from persevering toward wisdom that comes only with time.   Not giving up creates a seasoned entrepreneur who learns to make wise decisions.

I did not have the benefit of a mentor in my industry who guided me through the steps of becoming a successful entrepreneur in book publishing in my early business career. I had the benefit of making mistakes that would allow me to find what was right and wrong in business entrepreneurship.   In my lectures, I have told my audience that I have made every possible mistake that an entrepreneur can make. I've trusted the wrong people and I spent money in the wrong places. However, I learned from those mistakes and did not repeat those mistakes.

This memoir is just a small overview of my experience as an entrepreneur working to provide contributions of published works to an audience. Those works go beyond just book publishing. I have been involved with film production, TV broadcasting, and hosting radio shows. Media is a powerful tool to reach the public. I started at a time long before social media where it was a greater challenge to publish content and manage delivery to the audience.

My entrance into business and my work as an entrepreneur started at a time in the mid-1990s when computer technology and internet capability was not what you see today. The ability to research was left to traveling to libraries and purchasing books from a bookstore. To be successful and achieve a return on a return on investment, business decisions required knowing what was the right thing to do. Learning how to do that was successful because of the foundation of prior mistakes.

The technology of the early 1990's did not offer research abilities offered by today's internet. There was no way to get a review of trialed business ideas and understand rate of success for venture conquests. Today, an idea can be evaluated by reviews and analysis found on the internet. Back in the 1990's, a business venture was new to the entrepreneur. I envy today's entrepreneurs who did not have to go through the trial-and-error process that included in investing in mistakes. The life of an entrepreneur on a new venture is much safer economically than it was when I started my business venture.

There is caution to be used when using the internet. There is a lot of miss-information that must be filtered out to get to the right beneficial advice. Subscribing to content leads to spam emails that trick consumers and entrepreneurs into poor investment decisions.

Today's internet content that offers hope of riches are false. This is proven by investing in the required fee and working diligently to find that the promised income is not realized. If the hope offered were real, then everyone would be doing it. Those that don't invest are smart and wise. Those that do are ignorant and uninformed.

Researching on the internet wisely involve seeking forums that offer shared advice. Ignorant entrepreneurs ignore this advice because the truth of reality is not the same as advertised riches seen on websites. It's an old trick, but many still fall for false hopes and false promises. Experienced entrepreneurs learn that throwing money into unconfirmed promises do not work. They put more focus on ROI, or Return On Investment. The analysis of ROI comes from historical evidence proven to be fact. This requires patience to wait for being properly informed before acting.

A great example of false hopes come from investing in advertising that does not have proven return on investment. It's common and unfortunate. Many business owners have the belief that indiscriminately investment without any knowledgeable backing can be successful. Silly isn't it, but many business owners do this. Advertising investment works right and effectively when results are measurable and reported to produce an accountable ROI. Not all advertising has proven ROI. Some do and those that have proven ROI are the ones that should be used for investment. Many novice-entrepreneurs do not realize that there are two kinds of advertising. Ones that are effective and, of course, the others that are not.

For me in the early 1990s, the decision-making process as an entrepreneur was developed without the benefit of clouded judgment caused by today's technology including spam emails and social media confusion. There were no false promises from websites. internet technology back in the mid-1990s did not exist. However, being business savvy with an entrepreneurial spirit was required to achieve success. A lot of work and studying was necessary. I put focus on making decisions that were fact driven rather than learning by trial-and-error. The idea was to avoid as much error as possible.

My evolution as an entrepreneur involved long days and working through mistakes to achieve success. The benefit is that I learned along the way what works and what does not work in business. I also learned that it is not necessary to be a millionaire or filthy rich to be considered successful in business. I didn't know that in the beginning of my entrepreneurial experience, but I do now. I consider myself a successful entrepreneur, even though I am not a millionaire or extravagantly rich by any means. My experience is that of a persevering entrepreneur working through situations and learning how the world works. It is an evolutionary process that builds wisdom and a spirit of innovation.

My area of expertise is in the area of digital multimedia technology and entrepreneurial studies. It requires the tech savviness of computer technology as it pertains to applications on the internet. My success comes from finding creative innovative solutions that are cost free. I have the mindset that there is a cost free solution to every problem. There was a time when I made a mistake of thinking that just saw the problem it required a financial investment. There are so many resources on the web today that there is open source code and other free resources available to do what others pay for to have done. As an entrepreneur, I look for a return on investment and if the investment is zero then the return is guaranteed. Even if that return is a small financial number, I still consider it a success.

Benefits of Experience

Running a small business as an entrepreneur has its benefits as well as its challenges. You may have heard the expression: take the good with the bad. For me years ago, the challenges were greater than the benefits. The evolution of experience has now made the benefits outweigh the challenges. I now know what not to do and what to avoid because I have past examples to follow.

Some business people do not know that the decision not to do something or not to move forward with a decision can be the correct decision. My father told me that with everything, it must be done at the right time. It is possible to do the right thing at the wrong time. It is also possible to do the wrong thing at the right time. Success is demonstrated when you do the right thing at the right time. A decision is one thing, but the action on that decision is based on timing and there's the right timing for certain things to be done. This perhaps is one of the biggest lessons I learned as an entrepreneur.

So often I had taken actions on the wrong thing at the wrong time. Over time I learned how to make the right decisions however it would be at the wrong time. Now after more than two decades I make the right decisions at the right time. This is not something that you learn. It is a skill that you acquire.

Novice-entrepreneurs, as I was myself many years ago, have such a strong passion that it overrides patience to seek out knowledge to know what works and does not work in business adventurism. People new to business make wrong choices, trust the wrong people, and put their money in the wrong investments. Some of those detours away from success are based on actions that are good, but done at the wrong time. People miss doing the right thing at the right time. Instead they do it at the wrong time. They don't know it because they believe they are doing the right thing. They are, but it is at the wrong time. There is a right time for everything. Along the journey of entrepreneurship, there are many times of patience and waiting. It is a skill that is hard to have in the early stages of an entrepreneurial business adventure. The excitement pushes us forward off the cliff of logic and we plunge to our mistakes. As we become experienced, those jumps over the cliff are less frequent. The best advice is to know that those cliffs exist and waiting is a good course of action. It doesn't cost money to wait for the right timing.

On the flip side of the coin, there is a time to move fast. Technology, circumstances, resource availability changes fast.   In these situations, an action may need to be taken quickly. This is a case where the action is not relevant in the past and the future, but is relevant at the current time. If an ROI or other benefit is verifiable, then the action may be prudent to take. These are situations that are hard to figure out.   Very often, the instinct of experience helps with making these kinds of decisions.

Educational Benefit

For any successful career based entrepreneurial business venture to be successful, the foundation of education is necessary. As a faculty member of educational institutions, I have seen that what is considered an important course of study decades into the past may not be applicable in the future however the importance remains the same. It is important that the education plants the seeds that have relevancy for the future. There are many changes that affect the importance as to what is studied in an educational institution. For example, this study of computers at the high school level in the 1970s is not the same as the study of computers in high school during present day.

For me, I was fortunate to have had a computer in 1979 during my senior year of high school which my father provided me during Christmas so that I could be accustomed to evolving technology. This was at a time that the term PC for personal computer didn't exist. It was also before the time when the standard IBM computer or Apple computer existed. It was a TRS-80 model one that was purchased at RadioShack ®. Of course, there was no windows or Microsoft Office. Imagine a high school student in 1979 with their own computer. That might seem normal as elementary students use laptops today, but back in 1979, it was unheard of. For me it provided a glimpse of technology of the future and the concept of having a computer being commonplace. In some ways this blessing was ahead of my time in 1979.

My undergraduate studies at the University of Massachusetts involved a major in mathematics and a minor in computer science. Mathematics helped me to understand the language of technology and computer science help me understand technology. This helped me form and understanding of technology and that foundation has help me throughout my career.

My graduate degree is in education. In 1988, I earned a master's degree in education at Cambridge College in Cambridge Massachusetts. (M.Ed.) That education taught me the various ways people receive and absorb information. My master's thesis was based on the topic of the relationship between teacher and student with education as the medium. I reported that some people like to be told how to do something; others like to be shown; while others like to learn by doing. I called it "tell, show, do". Later, this master's degree and my thesis work would prove to be valuable in my entrepreneurial efforts in communication via publishing, broadcasting, and public speaking.

In my early entrepreneurial career, I was immersed in the art of book publishing. I called it an art, because it involved literature and a pretty thing on a bookshelf. In later years, publishing would go digital and be immersed in the world of technology. This is something I was well versed in and was able to handle comfortably the evolution of the industry I began in. I would say around the year 2000 is when book publishing took a turn toward a world of technology. Before Amazon had a foothold, the first set of ereaders emerged in 1998 such as the Rocket Ebook and SoftBook Reader. A year later the EveryBook Reader and Millenium Ebook reader emerged. Amazon released their first generation of the

Kindle on November 19, 2007. This is when the idea of ereaders took off. It took 9 years from the first product for another company to gain foothold. This is because it took that long for the consumer population to begin accepting ebooks as another medium. The early inventers had a great idea in 1998, but it was about 9 years too early. Also Amazon had the brand name and marketing knowhow to launch this nine-year-old concept.

Memoir

When I am lecturing in front of an audience or broadcasting on radio, I usually tell a little bit about myself so that people have an understanding of the reason why I say what I say. So much has happened since the start of my entrepreneurial venture. In 1994, that it is difficult to explain my role in the various industries that I take part in. This memoir gives an opportunity to encapsulate a complete understanding of my entrepreneurial efforts along with the successful milestones along the way. it offers a true account of the evolution of my entrepreneurial efforts that begin in book publishing and expanded into digital multimedia technology spread across various Industries. It is a unique story as any memoir is that sheds light into historical experiences serving as a solid foundation that build confidence moving forward.

What is a memoir? A memoir explains the history of a person and describes how that history positions that person to make certain decisions. Those decisions formed a path in life that, at certain points, should be recognized by their work.

After 22 years in business, I thought it best to mark this occasion with a memoir that I feel is halfway through my voyage of entrepreneurship. In another 22 years, I will be 75 and may perhaps at that time retire from business ventures. I say perhaps. A lot can happen in 22 years as has already happened in the past 22 years.

This memoir is a reflection of the past 22 years as an entrepreneur and a business strategist in the digital multimedia industry. For about half of those 22 years, I spent 11 years as a subject matter expert in the industry by lecturing at universities and colleges in the 7 states of New York and New England. In addition, I have written and published many books on the subject.

With experience, I can share knowledge, but cannot put experience in one person's head. If that were true, then it would be so easy to have my experiences prevent others from making the mistakes I've made. Unfortunately, people are left to their own preferences and therefore decisions that are misguided. I've learned to sit and watch and accept the natural course of learning evolution that involves mistakes. I wish I had been guided. I've told my students at universities that I wish I had someone who would guide me. I was alone due to the technologies that was available. The workshop seminars weren't available, which is why I created 18 of them and toured the seven states of New York and New England at 52 education institutions from 2004 to 2015 (11 years).

A memoir is the best way to share experiences in addition to knowledge.   This book and audiobook serve as my lecture related to insight evolved from experience. Perhaps this opportunity will save others from investing in the wrong solutions that are based on wrong perceptions and false gut feelings.

At this juncture in my entrepreneurial career, it is best to reflect on the successes that I have been blessed with so that understand its true meaning and purpose so that I can make the next 22 years more effective and productive than the last 22 years.

Intended Legacy

Nobody lives forever in a physical life in a human body on Earth. That being said the goal of most people who want to fulfill a purpose desire to leave a legacy behind for future generations.   My goal is to leave and entrepreneurial legacy that will benefit future generations. This is one such legacy that I intend to leave behind that is career specific. It is not the only legacy I plan to leave behind. God has a purpose for me. This presentation is a discussion that is specific to a career paste entrepreneurial legacy.

I will give you an example of a career based entrepreneurial legacy that I observed left behind by a man I admire and love you so much. My father was the one who discovered that hydrogen exist in space. This was due to his development and work of radio telescopes that could detect the hydrogen line in space. My father's exploration of the universe using radio astronomy has resulted in an ever lasting legacy in the scientific community.

The kind of career based entrepreneurial legacy that I want to leave behind is one that has provided a contribution resulting in a positive impact that is felt by future generations. That sounds powerful, but it is what I want to deliver. After 22 years of hard work and pouring out, why wouldn't I? A legacy is a tangible piece of evidence that supports the value and benefit of a person's contribution. My hope end goal is to have a career based entrepreneurial legacy that is carried through future generations because of seeds planted build a strong foundation in my entrepreneurial area of expertise in the industry that I have put such great attention into. In many ways, a legacy has already been left behind. In many ways, I want to do more. Either way, the legacy is a gift to the world I live in. It is not something to be boastful of. It is not driven by pride. It is not evolved from the wrong things. A legacy offers solutions, hope, prosperity for future generations. If I can offer more of that, then I would have accomplished providing a contribution in the world I live in.

Who is David K. Ewen, M.Ed.

I normally introduce myself as an author, speaker, and talk show host. These characteristics describe me as a person who works with people and networks with a community of industry members. Without saying it, I am also a record producer, filmmaker, broadcaster, journalist, and educational ambassador. Running a business immersed in technology, a business market, and the general public has thrown various opportunities my way. A true blessing.

My initial career background is very much different from the way I introduce myself. My undergraduate studies at the University of Massachusetts in Amherst was mathematics with a computer science concentration. A few years later I earned a master's degree in education.

For about the first 15 years of my career, I work as an information technology industry specialist at data centers for a bank (BayBank Systems, Inc.) and a mutual fund company (Putnam Investments). I specialized in the backup and recovery of systems in Disaster Recovery scenarios. Back then, during the years of 1985 to the year 2000, when I worked in the industry as a systems programmer, the idea of Disaster Recovery as an investment by a company was not taken as seriously as it should have been. This helped me later to transition into call center management to transformed me from an individual contributor to a business leader in middle management.

As I said before, disaster recovery was not taken seriously in the last 15 years of the previous century as it should have been. Today with a larger number of natural disasters and terrorist activities seen in the news, it is apparent that Disaster Recovery planning has significant importance for organizations.

As a systems programmer I worked on business recovery plans and Datacenter Disaster Recovery plans. I conducted multiple tests of data center recovery with me standing on a computer room floor for 32 hours straight. Yes, 32 hours of focused work on a computer room floor. I took the work seriously and learned a tremendous amount of systems and application programming. I found that Disaster Recovery coordinators had the job of knowing everything and that gave me the opportunity to learn a lot about the industry.

Those days, the big IBM mainframe was a common data processing and information technology infrastructure that companies had. Today, it is more cloud-based with a distributed server environment relying less on the legacy mainframes. Connectivity is app driven on mobile devices and other mobile office technology.

I spend time to explain my technical background because it has huge relevance in my book publishing experience. Many of the book publishers I had worked with have fallen off to the side because they could not keep up with the technology evolving. The understanding of ebooks and audiobooks as they evolved seem to mystify former book publishing professionals. Granted audiobooks had been around for many years but it is the recent ubiquitous nature of mobile devices that has given a new explosion of growth for audio books. When the digital content delivery book publishing came about I remember saying to myself "Now they are talking my language".

In today's world, the self-publishing in the independent press industry relies heavily on the individual understanding digital multimedia technology for them to succeed not only in physical book publishing, but also the digital content delivery of ebooks and audiobooks. I have told by audience members in my more recent lectures that book publishing is not just a pretty paper thing sitting on a shelf. It involves mobile devices, smartphones, and tablet computers that everyone carries and is connected to the cloud. The self-published authors of today need to be savvy of digital multimedia content delivery. this is no longer a hardcover book with printed pages sitting on a wooden Shelf.

Up until the time I started in book publishing in the year 1994, book publishing was an antiquated art. It was called an art because of the way books were manufactured and printed. The art involved the cover, the materials used, the font, the design of the book, the glue, the stitching.

Book publishing involved the physical manufacturing of a product that involved materials associated with paper, glue, ink, and binding materials. The elements would be put together in an attractive way that would appeal to the consumer audience.

Today's book publishing eliminates all of the manufacturing of a physical product and is doing more today with digital multimedia content such as ebooks and audiobooks.

Story of Paper Books

People ask me how ebooks play a role in book publishing and if paperback books are going away. I won't go as far as to say that paperback books are going away. People still love the tactile feel and smell of physical books. I believe they are staying. When television came about, it did not make radio go away. As a matter of fact, radio has expanded from broadcast to satellite and internet. Granted television is bigger than radio but radio did not go away. It actually grew. Let's look closer at the media of radio for a moment. Not only did TV not make radio go away, but radio did not make the newspaper go away. As new technologies emerge, the old ones do not go away. Instead they evolve and position themselves to fit better into a new evolving market. The same is true with paperback books with the introduction of ebooks. Audiobooks are being reintroduced as the improved delivery using mobile devices has helped this media. So, in short, ebooks are an addition to paperback books; not a replacement. The same holds true for audiobooks.

Now when my attention is on book publishing, I no longer think of just the paperback book. Ebooks has thrown me into a greater use of social media to deliver content. the production of audiobooks got me involved with music production. Just the nature of book publishing today requires digital multimedia expertise. There are a lot of technologies to work with beyond printed words on paper.

Today when I publish books, they are produced as a paperback book, an ebook, and an audiobook. They are found on Amazon, Barnes & Noble, and many other online outlets. Now I'm working on developing simple ways to get a book produced as some sort of video book or a simplified way of a converted written piece of work in video format. The technology with a cost exists today. What I'm working on is a cost effective or free methodology. Of course it is possible and has been done before but it needs to be done in efficient optimize fashion that offers a return on investment.   I am not satisfied that the only way to create video-book content requires financial investment with an unknown risk that may not offer a return on investment.

Ewen Prime Company

Ewen Prime Company was founded on July 24th 1994 at 11:30 AM in Natick, Massachusetts. The internet technology back in those days was not the same as it is today. The study and research of the industry required me purchasing books and also going to the public library and researching. As a single bachelor, I had a significant amount of time invested in the study of an industry that I got into without any prior knowledge.

My original involvement in the book publishing industry was to create a product rather than a service. The investigative efforts started in 1993 (year before launch of business) when I was working with a potential partner to create a desktop publishing service two people needing help with their resume or other simple documentation.

The idea would be to create a business offering a service instead of a product. Imagine what the technology was like in 1993. Fortunately, back then I was able to discern and foresee that the technology emerging indicated more people will be producing documents on their own. That is when I decided to produce a product instead of offering a service. So instead of creating documents for people, I chose to publish books.

The way my company, Ewen Prime Company, started was not involved with me writing a book. Many small publishing companies do start that way. I did not get into publishing as an author. As I've told my audience members in lectures, I am a project manager by trade and focus on the operations of a business. I work better as an operations manager leading a staff. This is what I had been good at since 1985. The experience carried through to the beginnings of Ewen Prime company. This is unique in that many small publishing houses begin with an author.   This wasn't the case for Ewen Prime company founded in 1994.

I hired writers, editors, and illustrators to produce books. There were two genres that we focused on. One was poetry and the other one was children's books. The most successful poetry book was Blue Poetry and the most successful children's book was called The Doll House. For the book Blue Poetry, I hired a college intern for illustrations and paid a flat rate. She was an art major at a local college.   The illustrator for The Doll House came from a friend of a friend. Both illustrators were fantastic and had a lasting effect on Ewen Prime Company.

The Doll House was written by a 17-year-old author who sold 197 books at the very first book signing. It was a huge publicity event put together. A huge feature article in the local paper covered the front and back side of an entire page. Never have I seen before a local author get coverage in the newspaper that's spread across the front and back of an entire piece of paper in the newspaper. It was totally amazing. As if that wasn't enough, she received an accommodation award recognizing her accomplishment of publishing a book at a young age.

The published work by the 17-year-old author and the marketing that followed is what kept the Publishing Company alive. Had that opportunity not happen, the company would have surely folded and my confidence and success in the independent publishing arena would have vanished. Fortunately, that did not happen and other success stories followed. By the way, that author is all grown up and now she's a college graduate who is married with two kids. Imagine that!

In 1994, Ewen Prime Company originally started in the living room of my one-bedroom apartment before being moved to commercial property in Natick, Massachusetts. That facility had a lobby, an office, and a conference room. That conference room was used to launch the New England Publishers Association (NEPA) that was a division of Ewen Prime Company in 1998. The early years of the business was in the area of book publishing and marketing. NEPA was created as a marketing mechanism that drove the self-publishing and independent press industry in New England. This was a creative innovation for a time such as the late 1990s.

After rapid expansion, two facilities were necessary to support our growing needs. One was office space that included a presentation meeting room for lectures. This was located in Westborough, Massachusetts on Route 9, Turnpike Road. The other one was around the corner from the original facility in Natick and served as a warehouse for books that were being presented to book fairs and festivals. Back then the only book product that was created more commonly was physical hardcover and paperback books. This was long before the concept of ebooks was developed. Audiobooks were on cassette tapes and could not be adequately stored in a warehouse. The audiobook industry was left to the large publishing powerhouses of the day.

In later iterations of Ewen Prime Company, when a staff was no longer required and clients weren't seen face to face, it was not necessary to have office facilities to invest in. Very often I would meet with people at coffee shops that had comfortable chairs and a nice seating arrangement that fit well for meetings. This type of meeting arrangement is commonly seen today however I adopted the concept back in the late 1990s. Perhaps I may have been one of the many earlier entrepreneurs who introduced the idea of using coffee shops as a place for business meetings.

Today it is very common to use web conferencing as a more convenient meeting venue. This technology did not exist back when I had started my entrepreneurial voyage in the 1990s.

Not many people are aware of the physical presence that Ewen Prime head with commercial real estate properties in Natick and Westborough, Massachusetts. This physical presence was long before the international presence that is enjoyed today. The technology of web conferencing allows for communication via internet vehicles that were not in existence so many years ago.

Other Businesses

Ewen Prime Company Started as a publishing house producing books, but as an entrepreneurial vehicle of exploration there have been many industries and trades that the company has explored. All of these have operated as a division of the parent company Ewen Prime Company.

Boston Voyager was the first division of Ewen Prime Company to serve as the desktop publishing service provider making large fold out brochures. This division was developed for temporary services offered to another organization.

The New England Publishers Association (NEPA) is the most successful division in the 1990s that Ewen Prime

Company had. It launched the very first trade association environment that supported self-publishers and the independent press industry in the six states of New England. The organization continues to grow under new ownership under the name of Independent Publishers of New England.

In the following century, Forest Academy was the most successful division of Ewen Prime Company. This supported the lecture tour in the seven states of New York and New England region at 52 educational institutions for 11 years. The tour, primarily held at universities and colleges, was called the Professor Lecture Series. It ran from July 2004 to August 2015.

On June 1st 2011, there was a tornado that ripped through Springfield Massachusetts and surrounding communities. Ewen Prime Company launch the

Springfield Community Festival that following September and opened the doors at the Bing Arts Center in Springfield Massachusetts as a free event. This gave an opportunity for the local community to take a break from the recovery efforts following this unusually rare tornado weather event. This initiative was featured in all the local television networks and all the local newspapers. The success created opportunities to run the festival a few more times over 2 years with the same level of media attention.

Your World Discovered, founded in 2009, is a division that supports films and movies that are on Amazon and local art centers. They have also been presented on other venues that include television. The original experience helped me to create a successful film festival, that followed the June 1st 2011 tornado, called the Springfield Community Festival.

To support a local community in my increase faith and walk with the Lord, the Resurrection Center was launched in 2012 as a division of Ewen Prime Company. The idea and design was not mine. My role was to provide a fast legal installation of a church that I had a strong belief in. I was not the pastor of the church, but supported wonderful pastors who needed to have a legally compliant church. This operated for a year-and-a-half before being spun off into a separate corporate entity that continues to thrive. The team and agents at Ewen prime Company administered the spinoff. The purpose was to create a legal and well-structured church that was compliant to every letter of the law. Ewen Prime Company sold the division for $1 and spun off the Resurrection Center as its own private corporate entity under the name of New Resurrection Center of Springfield, Inc. Under the excellent leadership and obedience to the Lord, the pastors have worked hard and obediently to the Lord to make the Resurrection Center continue to grow. Today, it is forgotten how the Resurrection Center was formed, but I am pleased to have had a small part that provided benefit.

EPN & EPN News is a feature article content development engine issuing content globally. Articles were released through the country of India two English-speaking Nations in the UK, Australia, Canada, and the United States. This initiative was launched in December 2013 and was the first international experience through the country of India. This experience continued through the fall of 2015. EPN is designated as Ewen Prime Network and encompasses a digital network of feature presentations that are written or in other formats produced by Your World Discovered (founded 2009)

The only business that did not form as a division of Ewen Prime Company is Kelvin Projects which served as an engineering firm during the summer of 2012. The purpose was to support the completion of an engineering project and serve as a flight engineer. Having originally studied electrical engineering during my undergrad career at the University of Massachusetts in Amherst, it was good to dabble a little bit with engineering to some small degree. My education at the university completed with a major in mathematics with a concentration in computer science. I didn't finish with a completed study or major in electrical engineering as I couldn't get past circuit analysis successfully. I graduated in mathematics and let electrical engineering behind. Kelvin Projects helped fulfill some success in this area about 27 years after the college experience.

The business model of launching divisions from the parent company has been commonplace for many years. It allows a tentacle of a company to explore different areas of entrepreneurship. Ewen Prime Company was launched as a vehicle of entrepreneurial exploration and its various divisions propelled that mission.

The most recent and latest division of Ewen Prime Company was the aforementioned Resurrection Center. It is suspected that this will not be the last entrepreneurial exploration into a new venture by the company. There will be other times when I'll assist others or venture into new areas as part of entrepreneurial exploration.

Broadcasting Ventures

Although not originally designed to be part of a business venture, my experience in broadcasting is varied. When I was running the New England Publishers Association, I fell into radio broadcasting by chance when trying to route members of the New England Publishers Association (founded in 1998) to a radio station. The program director suggested that I be the host. That is how I broadcasted a weekly radio show from 9:00 am to 10:00 am on WORC 1310 AM and WGFP 940 AM every Thursday morning before going into ABC News. The LIVE show was a simulcast broadcast on both radio stations. One was in Worcester, Massachusetts (WORC 1310 AM) and the other was in Webster, Massachusetts

(WGPF 940 AM). I was broadcasting out of Studio B in Webster.

An interesting note about WORC 1310 AM is that it was the very first station to air music play a song from the famous Beatles band. The song was on a Golden Record from Swan Records and called "She Loves You". The following year, the Beatles were on the Ed Sullivan TV show when their fame was finally launched. WORC 1310 AM launched in 1995 and was New England's very first Rock and Roll station.

I am honored to have been a talk show host on WORC 1310 AM airing my show "Author of The Week" on such a famous historic radio station that is still in existence today.

Long before satellite and internet radio became popular, I had produced and hosted today's music review that was recorded in Connecticut and aired in Los Angeles, California. It aired every Monday morning from 11:30 a.m. to noon in Los Angeles California. This was the first time my voice reached across the nation. It was not too long after I was married in 2002. My wife came with me to the studios in Connecticut for a taping of "Today's Music Review". I interviewed New England bands and played music. This would give new bands coast-to-coast exposure and recognition.

When internet radio came about, I became a host on Blog Talk Radio within their first year of existence. I was one of their original talk show hosts who served as a guest on their first anniversary show. My show was called "Today's Author" and ran for several years. On the same platform, I produced 5 different radio shows for Circle of Seven Productions in 2009:

- Monday: Book Bridge, From Authors to Readers
- Tuesday: Canned Laughter and Coffee
- Wednesday: Book World News
- Thursday: Today's Author
- Friday: Reader's Entertainment Radio

I originally hosted the shows on Monday and Tuesday until later full-time host where assigned.   I continue to produce all five shows and hosted the Wednesday, Thursday, and Friday shows.

The Blog Talk Radio audio content was merged to a collage and montage of pictures and images to make a local community access television show. I blended the recording of the Blog Talk Radio broadcast with a nice portfolio of images. This was and additional experience of utilizing community access television for broadcasting. The broadcast was on channel 12 from Focus Springfield. Originally, the station was part of Comcast, one of the largest telecommunication companies in the United States.

My original television broadcast started in 1998 as a pilot for "Author of the Week" which was a spinoff of the weekly radio broadcast on WORC 1310 AM and WGFP 940 AM radio stations. The broadcast ran on WCAT out of Westborough, Massachusetts. The station was called the CAT Studios of Westborough.

Over the years, my experience in broadcast television came into play by chance via national media attention. There was one time I was interviewed on NBC Nightly News and another time by the Weather Channel with a featured interview in the Bahamas when Hurricane Irene was coming. These experiences and others inspired me to do more in the area of video production and lecturing on the topic of television and film making. In 2012 and the following few years I put great attention in a weekly broadcast of a church service from the Resurrection Center in Springfield Massachusetts. This continued for a few short years until the time commitment could not be continued. I found that video production for TV and filmmaking is significantly larger and requires more resources than radio or any other type of audio content.

More recently I have been taking the experience of book publishing and radio broadcasting and combining them into audio book publishing. Because of the evolution of mobile devices, the audiobook industry is growing. this has caused greater attention into my production audio books. This experience draws in from the resource of knowledge gained from music production and marketing.

The Early Years

The early years were simple. Ewen Prime Company was a vehicle of exploration of an industry that was still developing. respecting the authenticity of the self-published author in the independent press industry had not yet been realized at the time of the founding of Ewen Prime Company. Because of that, it was a challenge. At the time I did not know that was the biggest challenge. I had thought it was because of my lack of knowledge in running a business. Although that played a role I was not fully aware that I was helping build the authenticity and respect for the self-published author and the independent press industry. Basically I was competing against the giant publishers in America. I did not know that and it was not my intent. I say that I was competing against those giant Publishers because they were the only ones that were recognized as I recognized publisher.

I had the attitude that the self-publishing and the independent press industry could be successful and I just had to find out how to make it happen. As a new start of business they were limited Financial Resources beyond my own personal investment. I was not in a position to use the resources that larger publishers invest in. I had to be creative and innovative with the way I manufactured, distributed, and marketed books.

Many things I learned on my own and created methods of getting things accomplished without having the benefit of an experienced mentor to guide me. I created a template design for books that would have a trim size of 5.5 by 8.5. I continue to use this template today as it has been successful for more than two decades.

The manufacturing of the product included laminated covers and comb binding of books with a trim size of 5.5 by 8.5. I manually bound all books and laminated the covers. With a camera, I created the graphic image used for the cover. I created covers for successful paperback books including The Doll House and Blue Poetry.

My award-winning author who wrote the book The Doll House had a photograph of the doll house she had grown up with built by her father. Several shots had to be taken because it took an effort to get the author's big fluffy dog to stay still while sitting in front of the doll house.

The cover of blue poetry was a photograph of the ocean and the sky meeting with seagulls flying in the scenery. I remember chasing the seagulls to get them to run and try to position myself so that the seagulls would be in view as I took a picture of the ocean connecting with the sky. Nearly 20 years after this book published I still have an enlargement blown up picture of the cover photograph of the cover for Blue Poetry that is framed and protected with museum glass. I remember giving the author the same picture and he had placed it prominently above his fireplace in the living room of his house with a light shining on it.

I never considered myself a very fancy graphic design artist. However, I am proud of the photographs taken that were used for books that were published by Ewen Prime Company and sold successfully.

The idea of using comb-binding work well for poetry and children's books. With this style of manufacturing it was best to stick with these two generous. The handmade books were of good quality, but not the quality that would be accepted in mainstream book stores. The way the books were marketed was through book signings that were conducted at the book stores. In the early years of Ewen Prime Company, the books were sold at events in the Boston area and as far north as Nashua, New Hampshire. That was the bookselling territory that was made available through author signings back in the 1990's.

To learn more and rub elbows with experts in the industry, that is when I founded the New England Publishers Association (NEPA) in 1998. The organization was launched in May 1998 at the offices of Ewen Prime Company. That was nearly four years after the launch of Ewen Prime Company in 1994. The trade Association was run as a successful profitable division of the Ewen Prime Company for two years before being sold.

When the New England Publishers Association was sold in the year 2000 it would be four years later that the Professor Lecture Series would be launched which would include the lecture publish your book guaranteed. That letter would go for 11 years in the 7 states of New York and New England.

The early years involved learning and growing that spawned into becoming an authority on the subject of self-published authors and the independent press industry. That in turn spawned into the expansion of other digital multimedia content publishing, distribution, and marketing. That includes broadcasting, music album production, film production, talk show hosting, and more. Ewen Prime Company is no longer just a publishing company. It is now a digital multimedia company under the moniker Forest Academy where educational resources are provided. The original territory was New York and New England. Today it is the United States, Japan, China, and the Middle East.

Forest Academy

Forest Academy launched on June 12th 2004 with the first lecture at Holyoke Community College in Holyoke Massachusetts. This moniker encompasses all of the lectures during the tour called the Professor Lecture Series from the years 2004 to 2015. The conclusion of the tour was in August of 2015 and expanded to the 7 states of New York and New England 52 different educational institutions and venues.

In addition to the tour, Forest Academy was also the central location where people could learn about the books published and other entrepreneurial studies.

Following the Professor Lecture Series tour, Forest Academy became the foundation of an educational and ambassadorship to Japan, China, and the Middle East. Written content development began in India in December of 2013. On June 22nd, Japan educational opportunities were presented in 2014. On August of 2013, China was added to the mix at the same time Saudi Arabia was.

Today the primary educational ambassadorship responsibilities involve Japan, China, and the Middle East. there are occasional opportunities in other countries as well.

Professor Lecture Series

The lecture "Publish Your Book Guaranteed" began on Saturday June 12, 2004 at Holyoke Community College in Massachusetts. Back then, the book publishing that I had experienced so far involve the production of paperback book that would be made available to the public in physical stores and libraries.

It was found that other media outside of book publishing could be produced using digital tools and marketed in similar fashion. This gave birth to the Professor Lecture Series that included book publishing and other digital media formats that involved audio and video. In fact, book publishing evolved from paper to electronic formats to audio. In the final years, of the Professor Lecture

Series the topic of audiobook production was included as part of the lecture Publish Your Book Guaranteed.

In subsequent iterations of this lecture there was evolution towards online sales an ebook development. Toward the end of the 11-year tour that included Publish Your Book Guaranteed, the lecture included audiobook publishing.

To fully experience the digital multimedia experience, the Professor Lecture Series included topics in the areas of radio broadcasting,
film production, and other topics related to journalism, broadcasting, and streaming online.

When the speaking tour ended in August of 2015, it was important to have the Professor Lecture Series continue in another format. A book series and audiobook series was produced to ensure that the Professor Lecture Series experience eternity and availability to a consumer population.

<u>Being Thankful</u>

It is estimated that during the 11 years of the Professor Lecture Series, a total of 25,000 miles was travelled by car within the 7 states of New York and New England reaching a population of thousands of attendees. as I've said to all of them they could have spent their weekday evenings or Saturday mornings anywhere else but chose to attend a lecture that was part of the Professor Lecture Series. this focus on learning and growth has shown me help people evolve in their intellectual capabilities. It involves commitment.

I dedicate the Professor Lecture Series to all the men, women, and children who have attended my lectures and in many cases on more than one occasion. Because they asked challenging questions, they have pushed me to be better at what I do in the industry that I work in.

Being an adjunct lecturer at colleges and universities throughout New York and New England has put me in front of an audience who have the expectation that my professional experience provides enlightenment and benefit to their goals. The tour was built on being engaged in Workforce Development and continuing education programs at colleges, universities, and other educational institutions. Most workshops seminars that were presented were held on a Monday through Thursday evening or Saturday morning for 3 hours. At the end of those three hours the attendees wrote an evaluation for my performance. The continued exceptional evaluations allowed me to continue coming back to the venues for 11 years. I took the challenge of meeting the expectations of my attendees seriously.

Moving forward, my goal is to continue in the serious effort to satisfy the enrichment needs of an audience looking to produce content and market it to the general public. My lecture tour involved an average of a four-hour round-trip that was done for each lecture. Using the platform, of audiobook publishing for presenting the Professor Lecture Series, I am able to reach a greater audience not possible by physical travel within the confines of the seven states of New York and New England.

Knowing My Audience

During my lecture series I always arrived in the lecture hall an hour early to set up the room and to greet my audience who arrived early. My lectures involved a meet-and-greet session that was before the start of the lecture and after the lecture ended. My audience got to know me very well during these important times.

The question I would always ask is, "When You saw this lecture list it what made you say I need to go to this and attend. What drove you to pay for the lecture and be here early?" Over the years, I found general consistency of what my audience was looking for. My success was based on knowing what my audience was looking for. For each lecture, the needs of the audience had slight differences. This was due to demographics and geographics and I became acutely aware of them in the 7 states of New York and New England. I knew my territory well.

Because I asked my audience what they expected to get in terms of knowledge and enlightenment before the end of the lecture, I was able to custom tailor the content to be directly related to what the audience was looking for. Over the years I got to be very good at satisfying the needs of my audience. this is how I consistently received excellent written evaluations that prompted my return to the venue regularly for 11 years straight.

My staff

For most of the nearly quarter Century that I have been in business, I have managed a freelance staff that included editors, illustrators, and writers.   I have enjoyed working with all of them. my career working for other companies help me understand the best practices of managing a staff. This first started 9 years before Ewen Prime Company was launched.   I had a head start in managing a business starting in 1985.   Ewen Prime Company was launched in the summer of 1994 (July 22).

More recently I have taken on clients and freelance my skills and services to other individuals and companies. My most recent efforts are international in nature supporting clients in the USA, Japan, China, and the Middle East.   my goal is to spread to other continents.

This expansion has help me become an educational ambassadors representing the United States by providing an understanding of the American lifestyle.

Honored to Meet People

There are so many things to be thankful for that the publishing industry has given me. Without it I would not have built a radio career that taught me other media Outlets and marketing skills. The opportunity to be the director of a major trade Association would not have been possible. Both speaking tours with a cumulative 12 years combined would not have happened. the opportunity to publicly speak and lecture at colleges and universities in the 7 states of New York and New England would not have happened.

So many countless notable people have come into my life who were totally amazing. I remember meeting former Secretary of Defense Caspar Weinberger (the 15th

United States Secretary of Defense) in New York at the small press book fair with his wife, Jane, who owned a publishing company (Windswept House Publishers, founded in 1984). Later, I met his son in Augusta, Maine while I was on a speaking tour. on my radio broadcast I met two astronauts. Dr. Edgar Mitchell was the sixth man to walk on the moon. Dr. Thomas D Jones flew four space shuttle missions. I also met many high-level leaders in the publishing industry either in person or when they were a guest on my radio broadcast.

Today's digital multimedia technology in conjunction with social media offers new ways for people to connect with each other. When I was in publishing in my earlier years the only way to network with the public is to physically be with them in person or by way of a radio broadcast. My connection with people involved publicly speaking to a LIVE audience at a workshop seminar while on tour or on a radio broadcast. as a publisher I attended many of the book signing events that my contracted authors held.   One of those authors was an award-winning author who received an accommodation from her home City for publishing a book at a young age. On the debut of her book she had a feature article in the local newspapers that covered the front and back of an entire page of a newspaper. I've never seen that happen before or ever again since then.

There was another time that I recognized that a major national Bookseller store had appreciation for The Works being published by company, Ewen Prime Company. I was with an author at a book signing in Nashua New Hampshire and a store employee approach the book signing table and ask to see the book.   While the author was busy signing books, I saw the employee walk down the aisle with the book and go around the corner. I couldn't believe it. We actually produced a book that was worth stealing by an employee of a national bookseller.

Behind every success story there is hard work that goes into the foundation for that success story to happen. I've seen it all and I've gone through the Blood Sweat and Tears to make it happen. During my lecture at colleges and universities, I would tell my audience that I've made all the mistakes and that my goal was to prevent them from making the same business mistakes as I did. You can learn a lot after more than two decades in book publishing. I've seen different angles of book publishing from manufacturing to marketing to broadcasting tutoring to trade events two lectures and much more.

Describing My Contribution

I normally start out my lectures by writing three things on a chalkboard or whiteboard. They are a question mark, dollar sign, and stick figure. Those three symbols would be on the board as my audience members arrive and are seated. They stare at those symbols wondering how I will incorporate those abstract symbols into the start of my lecture. I explain to them it is related to their future. The order of the figures from left to right are question mark, dollar sign, and stick figure.

These three symbols are representative of what their future is. This concept began with my lecture in book publishing. I would explain that there are three things that will stop you from getting your book published. I then point to the question mark, dollar sign, and stick figure. Next, I explain each one starting with the question mark, then the dollar sign then the stick figure.

There are three things that stop you from succeeding in doing something in life. The first one is knowing how to do it. The first symbol representing knowledge is the question mark. That issue or obstacle is addressed because the audience member is attending the lecture. By the time they leave the lecture, the audience will have all the knowledge resources needed to succeed.

The second symbol representing an obstacle in life is a dollar sign. The second thing that stops people from accomplishing something is related to cost. everything that I explained in the lecture Publish Your Book Guaranteed does not cost a thing. Everything that I share in the lecture has tips and ideas that do not cost a thing.

So far the first two symbols representing knowing how to do something and the cost to do something have been eliminated as barriers on how to get a book published. The lecture describes how to do it at zero cost.

The final figure is a stick figure of a person. I asked my audience members if they see the door that they entered the room left. They all turn and look. After they turn their heads back to me, I asked him to look at the door again. I explain to them that the only thing that's stopping them from publishing their book is themselves. It won't be knowing how to do it and it won't be related to cost. The only obstacle that will stop a person from publishing their book is themselves. I explain to my audience members that it won't be me personally that will stop them from publishing their book. Their own perceptions and misunderstandings of book publishing is what will stop them from getting their book published.

At the end of the lecture, I remind the audience members of the three symbols representing knowledge, cost, and personal obstacles. They recognize that they have the knowledge to get their book published at zero cost.

At the end of the lecture, I give a splash of reality and remind my audience members that I am mindful and fully aware that each of them is excited and eager about their project, however when they exit the door and the reality of life sets in, their own personal obstacles will try to get in the way of their book project. I tell my audience members that I know that and it's a reality. I asked them to be mindful of that and to make efforts to not let that happen.

As an audience member writes out an evaluation at the conclusion of a lecture, I pass out my business card that has my website. For those that want a book on the topic discussed or other topics that I let her run, the book is available online in both paperback and ebook. I presented published works in this fashion so that I would not have to carry a library of books as if I was running a bookmobile in the seven states of New York and New England.

I rest easy at night knowing that I gave an opportunity to thousands of audience members over the years to publish their book without the obstacle of not knowing how to do it and the obstacle of cost. The restrictions related to knowledge and money were eliminated from all audience members who sat in front of me as I lectured to them for three hours.

Over the Years

There were many incredible experiences that occurred during the 11-year tour in the 7 states of New York and New England. These unique experiences demonstrated that the effort was worth it and that it had value to my audience.

I remember one time I arrived at a community college in Connecticut an hour before the start of a Saturday morning lecture on a gloomy cold rainy day. There was a woman sitting outside of the lecture room. She introduced herself to me and explained that she had attended my publisher book guaranteed lecture a year prior. The woman explained to me that it was in her heart to take time out on a Saturday morning and look for me at the college to hand-deliver the book that she published. That truly touched my heart. On a gloomy rainy day on a Saturday morning she could have been anywhere else but she chose to seek me out on a college campus to bring her book to me. I remember that my eyes watered with tears.

In the spring of 2015, just nearing the end of my 11-year tour of the Professor Lecture Series, I addressed the faculty, staff, and students at Cambridge College in Cambridge Massachusetts. It was a two-hour lecture of my alma mater. It was in 1988 that I earned my master's degree in education at Cambridge College. It was 27 years after I graduated. This was a true honor to return "home" to address my alma mater.

When I was lecturing at Cambridge College to an audience of faculty, staff, and students, I recognize that one faculty member was truly focused on what was being presented. It was weeks later that she had published her book based on the information provided. She explained to me that she had gone to the publishing company that she had interned at and they were not able to help her. She was amazed that she could do the work herself rather than relying on the publishing company that she had interned at.

I was touched and honored that a success story as huge as this would come from my alma mater that I had graduated from with a master's degree in education more than a quarter of a century before period it was nice to come back home to the college and provide such a significant contribution. Two other women who attended the conference engaged conversation with me at the end and explained their confidence in getting their work published.

Making an Impact

There are so many other success stories that I am not even aware of because it has not been brought to my attention. I am mindful that some success stories are brought to my attention While others occur without me being aware of it. I believe that might 11-year tour in the 7 states of New York and New England at universities Kama colleges, and other educational institutions have had an impact on the independent book publishing community.

The Professor Lecture Series began in 2004. That was ten years after launching my publishing company called Ewen Prime Company. It was in May of 1988 that I launched the New England Publishers Association (NEPA) to pull six New England states together in a community of authors and independent publishers. This venture had many significant programs including workshops seminars that help build a network of independent New England publishers.

At the New England Publishers Association, we flew in subject matter experts well known in the industry into Boston to conduct full day workshops seminars in beautiful venues such as the luxurious Sheraton Tara Hotel in Framingham. People from all six New England states were invited and attended. they exchanged business cards and network with each other in person and later on line.

There was one event where we had Tom and Marilyn Ross who were the cofounders of the Small Publishers Association of North America (SPAN). While Tom was suffering from the flu in the hotel room, Marilyn

Ross continued with the full-day workshop seminar titled jumpstart your book sales. Later I spoke with Marilyn Ross at a private luncheon at the Sheraton Tara Hotel in Framingham where we discussed the future of the independent publisher's arena in New England.

Another time, I flew in Jim Cox of Midwest Book Review to conduct a full day workshop seminar titled, "Tips, Tricks, and Techniques to Getting Your Book Reviewed". It was his first time in Boston and for many years after his only time in Boston. I remember during the audience break where people got refreshments and exchanged business cards, Jim Cox said that was the most important part of the workshop seminar. Although his message was powerful, he believed as I did that the networking that occurred during workshop seminar conferences was critical for the growth of the independent publisher's industry.

Another notable time is when Mary Westheimer flew in from Scottsdale Arizona from her company BookZone to talk about the internet presence of authors and publishers using websites. This was in the year 1998 at a time when websites for individuals and small businesses was considered futuristic. BookZone had created the first iteration of the website for the New England Publishers Association. I had created a website using Yahoo's "geocities" platform to create a website for Ewen Prime Company.

There were other projects and special guests speaking that developed the networking of authors and independent publishers. the New England Publishers Association change the landscape of the independent publishing community and built a networking environment at an early stage of the internet in 1998.

Much greater internet networking capabilities such as Facebook did not exist. The New England Publishers Association begin at the tail end of the century in 1998. it would be six years later in the year 2004 that Facebook would be launched. It is incredible what was accomplished without the benefit of today's common social media networking tools.

Other Media Outlets

As part of the marketing efforts given cost-free to authors at the New England Publishers Association, a radio shows on WORC 1310 AM and WGFP 940 AM broadcasted every Thursday morning from 9 to 10 a.m. before going into ABC News. The two radio towers for broadcasting the show "Author of the Week" from Webster Massachusetts and Worcester Massachusetts. This was a good central location in New England that fit well to support an organization called the New England Publishers Association. These radio shows later spawned into the pilot of a community access television program at the CAT studios in Westborough, Massachusetts (WCAT).

This venture into radio happened by accident. I was reaching radio stations to see who would interview authors who are members of the New England Publishers Association. One radio station manager said that I should interview the guests. This is how I began a radio career. WORC 1310 AM and WGPF 940 AM was my first broadcast experience. This later spawned to television.

To further support authors on radio, at a time much later, I became one of the original talk show host on Blog Talk Radio doing a show called "Today's Author". Later this was merged with Circle of Seven Radio where I produced five different radio shows on Blog Talk Radio.

The experience of broadcasting online radio supporting authors help me to understand help media played a role in marketing books. As a publisher, I was on one side of the fence and as a radio talk show host I was on the other side of the fence. I was in the unique situation to see both sides of the fence. The experience was unique and advantageous. This gave me the opportunity to lecture on publishing topics in a way that related directly to getting books into reader's hands. There are many publishers and there are many talk show hosts but there aren't many publishers who are also talk show host.

The First Tour

While running the New England Publishers Association (founded in 1998), I thought it was in my best interest to conduct a speaking tour to promote self-publishing and the independent press industry. Back then, there were two major bookstores that competed with each other. One was Borders Booksellers and the other was Barnes & Noble. Today, Borders is closed and Barnes & Noble remains in business. I conducted a year-long speaking tour at those two bookstores and at other venues to promote self-publishing and the independent press industry. This tour occurred during the time I was broadcasting the radio show on Thursday mornings. it was an active time for me as the founding director of the New England Publishers Association.

Being On the Map

The New England Publishers Association, along with the speaking tour and radio broadcast, put self-publishing and the independent press industry on the map. There was a solid foundation for people to recognize that self-publishing was possible and the independent press industry was real. Back in 1994 ('98 for NEPA), when this all started, the idea of book publishing was held only to the large powerful book publishers. Self-published authors and the independent press industry was not considered a real entity.

The efforts of the New England Publishers Association, the first speaking tour in the late 1990s, and the radio show created the solid foundation of self-publishing and the independent press industry. I firmly believe that New

England got its true start in the acceptance of self-publishing from this organization. Long before social media existed, the power of a speaking tour and radio broadcast in conjunction with the networking of the trade association like the New England Publishers Association gave birth to the acceptance and respect to authors who were self-published.

The New England Publishers Association was given prominence and recognition when it became an affiliate of the two largest publishing trade associations in America. Back then, they were called the Publisher's marketing Association (PMA) run by Jan Nathan and the other was the small Publishers Association of North America (SPAN) run by Tom and Marilyn Ross. We were represented at trade shows in Boston and New York selling our organization member's published books.

After the success of creating an impact of the publishing community, I sold the organization and stepped down as founding director so that other greater projects could begin. With the self-publishing and the independent press industry launched into acceptance in New England, it was time for others to take the reign. Today, the organization runs as the Independent Publishers of New England (IPNE). They continued on the foundation built by the New England Publishers Association (NEPA) years ago. I am proud of planting the seed to what is successful today.

This taught me that being a successful entrepreneur does that necessarily mean current activities as a business leader. Some of those activities can be successfully planted seeds for an outcome that is much greater in the future. One such example is the Independent Publishers of New England that originally started as the New

England Publishers Association back in 1998. In the year 2018 that effort will be 20 years old.

The Start of the Professor Lecture Series

It took two years to get a community college convinced that I had the ability to lecture on the topic of book publishing. This was back in 2002 when self-publishing in the independent press industry was not considered widely accepted. My efforts began in 2000. The title of the lecture was Published Your Book Guaranteed. Even the word "guaranteed" in scared the Dean. The idea of self-publishing books did not seem realistic to him.

After a two-year effort to set up a meeting, the Dean of Community Education of Holyoke Community College in Massachusetts and I had an energetic two-hour conversation. I was very transparent and held nothing back. I had nothing to lose. At the end of the meeting he expressed his appreciation and thankfulness that I was a bit forceful to ensure that the meeting take place because he finally saw the value of the lecture that I was offering at the community college. He fully accepted. That is what launched an 11-year lecture tour in New York and New England.

The acceptance of "Publisher Your Book Guaranteed" at Holyoke Community College in Massachusetts started a journey. This began the Professor Lecture Series that would eventually spread to the seven states of New York and New England at 52 venues for an 11-year period. The travel distance for this tour would be 25,000 miles, more than the equivalent of driving around the world.

I remember that the Dean of Community Education said that, after a few lectures, I would build a following. I didn't believe it at the time because I did not have the experience of lecturing at a college or university before.

As years passed, I found that to be true and I did build a following and it successfully spread through the seven states of New York and New England.

I have great appreciation for the opportunity given to me by the Dean of Community Education at Holyoke Community College. It was the first college I provided a lecture at and most importantly created the foundation for me to be accepted at other colleges and universities within Massachusetts. Later, that provided acceptance into other states reaching the seven states of New York and New England.

I will never forget the day. it was Saturday June 12th 2004 at Holyoke Community College. The lecture titled Publish Your Book Guaranteed ran from 9:00 a.m. to 1:00 p.m. on that Saturday. This was long before the idea of ebooks and audiobooks. Years later the topic of ebooks and audiobooks were added to the lecture and the lecture was reduced to three hours for efficiency and optimization of time as I was lecturing at many more colleges and universities.

It is important to note with the Dean of Community Education at Holyoke Community College had told me in a phone conversation many years after that very first lecture on the topic of book publishing. He told me that I was ahead of the curve in book publishing. That was his way of saying that for me to convince him that I could lecture on a topic that was ahead of the curve was an accomplishment. I thanked him for those kind words. This showed that he recognized that something new and creatively innovative was happening. it started at Holyoke Community College and spread to the seven states of New York and New England. This was a significant impact to the self-published author and the independent publishing community.

It is an interesting note that the word "guaranteed" for the lecture "Publish Your Book Guaranteed" could never be used as part of the title at any educational institution in Connecticut. This includes colleges and universities. I was speaking to a representative at Manchester Community College in Manchester Connecticut and talked to them about the publishing process with the testimony of attendee evaluations. Even in the agreement that the word guarantee was a valid title, they still did not accept the idea of putting guaranteed in the title. In Connecticut, I always told my audience that the true name of the lecture was published your book guaranteed.

The lecture "Publish Your Book Guaranteed" Was not accepted to be offered at a Boston Area Community

College because the director of continuing education expressed that what was being offered was too hard to believe. My response was I took her opinion as a compliment.

Out of the 18 lectures offered by Forest Academy, the lecture "Publish Your Book Guaranteed" was always considered my flagship offering to colleges and universities. It served as the foundation of other developed curriculum in the area of marketing, filmmaking, music recording, and more. It is also the one that holds the greatest experience.

Giving from The Heart

Entrepreneurs are business leaders and it is the responsibility of a leader to provide contributions to their community. At least that's how I felt when I first launched my business in the year 1994.

On June 1 2011 in the state of Massachusetts, there was an EF3 tornado that ripped through Springfield and surrounding communities. For many parts of the nation, the idea of an EF3 tornado is relatively common, but that isn't the case for Springfield, Massachusetts in New England. We were unprepared to recover from the damage emotionally at first from such a new event to our community.

Three months later, I rented a community arts center in the city and ran a film festival. We attracted a few filmmakers to provide short films to entertain the Springfield Massachusetts community at this arts center. We open the doors and let people come in free of charge to take a break from the recovery efforts of the tornado. It was a day to give peace to the community. It was so successful in featured locally on all television networks that I ran the festival a few more times as a free gift to the community.

Christian Influence

In simple terms the Bible teaches us the difference between what is right and what is wrong. I have told my pastors that the study of what is taught in church and learn from the Bible has help guide me in my decision making process as an entrepreneur in business. I find it incredibly amazing and rewarding that scriptures written thousands of years ago have relevancy to the practices of entrepreneurship and business enterprises. My hope is that other Business Leaders lean more towards the Bible as a safe haven away from core business decision-making.

More importantly than knowing how to run a business is knowing how to run your life. That is what the Bible in part intends to do. when individuals run their life correctly and according to the order of God and His will as intended then everything else falls into place. This includes being an entrepreneur and running a business.

Being a Christian has guided me towards successful avenues with the help of God along the way. The effectiveness comes from worship, tithing, fellowship, and church attendance. By incorporating all four of these elements, the natural process of improve decision-making and receiving a more fulfilling life automatically takes place. It is a Biblical principle. I wish more entrepreneurs would recognize this and enjoy the appreciation of what God has promised and offers everyone.

Relevant Scriptures

Deuteronomy 8:18 (NIV) But remember the LORD your God, for it is he who gives you the ability to produce wealth, and so confirms his covenant, which he swore to your ancestors, as it is today.

Joshua 1:9 (NIV) Have I not commanded you? Be strong and courageous. Do not be terrified; do not be discouraged, for the LORD your God will be with you wherever you go.

1 Peter 5:8 (NIV) Be alert and of sober mind. Your enemy the devil prowls around like a roaring lion looking for someone to devour.

Proverbs 2:6-8 (NIV) For the LORD gives wisdom; from his mouth come knowledge and understanding. He holds success in store for the upright, he is a shield to those whose walk is blameless, for he guards the course of the just and protects the way of his faithful ones.

Proverbs 29:11 (NIV) Fools give full vent to their rage, but the wise bring calm in the end. Watch your temper!

Ephesians 6:12 (NIV) For our struggle is not against flesh and blood, but against the rulers, against the authorities, against the powers of this dark world and against the spiritual forces of evil in the heavenly realms.

Philippians 3:13-14 (NIV) Brothers and sisters, I do not consider myself yet to have taken hold of it. But one thing I do: Forgetting what is behind and straining toward what is ahead, I press on toward the goal to win the prize for which God has called me heavenward in Christ Jesus.

This memoir recognizes the following scripture as being most prominent in the journey of entrepreneurship.

"For I know the plans I have for you," declares the Lord, "plans to prosper you and not to harm you, plans to give you hope and a future."

- Jeremiah 29:11 (NIV)

The Future

When I started on this entrepreneurial voyage nearly a quarter of a century ago, I did not know where it would leave go. A lot has happened that was rewarding and unexpected. As I look forward to the next quarter century, I can only guess, but I really do not know how the next chapter of this voyage will turn out. I do know that the journey will be exciting and the new opportunities of discovery will lead the way. I have always said Ewen Prime Company was a vehicle of exploration and of first nearly quarter century years has proven that. Without fear and hesitancy, Ewen Prime Company will continue to explore as part of an entrepreneurial voyage.

<u>Conclusion</u>

My hope is that a discussion of my entrepreneurial experience will shed light on what truly defines success in business without having to become wealthy. The purpose is to show that wealth does not define success. The best way to describe success is when you enjoy what you are doing and are good at it. Every entrepreneur has a parent or a mentor who always says to them I want you to be happy. That is what my parents said to me and that's what my pastors say to me. I can tell you that I am happy.

"For I know the plans I have for you," declares the Lord, "plans to prosper you and not to harm you, plans to give you hope and a future."

- Jeremiah 29:11 (NIV)

"I ask God to lead me toward the lasting legacy that He wants me to leave behind on this world we call Earth."

- David K., Ewen, M.Ed. (July 2016)

An Entrepreneur's Impact

A Memoir of Success

By:

David K. Ewen, M.Ed.

Ewen Prime Company

Forest Academy